Bas

GERI

Grammar

J. E. CLAPHAM

Head of Modern Languages, Sir Roger Manwood's School,
Sandwich

JOHN MURRAY

*I would like to dedicate this booklet to
the memory of one of my former pupils,
Roger Richards, who died at a tragically early age.
I hope that all who use it will work with the same industry
and enthusiasm that he did and also that they
may be granted a longer life than his, so that
they may enjoy the fruits of their learning.*

J.E.C.

First published 1971
Reprinted 1974, 1977, 1978, 1981

Printed in Hong Kong by
Wing King Tong

0 7195 2040 1

Contents

Section	Content	Page
1. Cases	Nominative	5
	Accusative	5
	Genitive	6
	Dative	6
2. Articles	Definite	8
	Indefinite	8
	Negative	8
	Demonstrative adjectives	8
	Derselbe	9
	Contractions of the definite article	9
	Special uses of the definite article	10
	Omission of the definite article	11
	Some, any	11
3. Verbs	Persons	12
	Present tense	12
	Imperfect tense	13
	Perfect tense	13
	Pluperfect tense	15
	Future tense	15
	Sein, haben and *werden*	15
	Strong and irregular weak verbs	17
	Subjunctive	22
	Modal verbs	23
	Compound verbs	26
	Reflexive verbs	27
	The passive	27
	The conditional	28
	Impersonal verbs	29
	Verbs governing the dative	29
	The dependent infinitive with and without *zu*	30
	Imperatives	31
	Present participles	32
	English verbal forms in -ing	32
	Tenses after *seit*	34

4. **Adjectives**	Agreement of adjectives	35
	Comparative and superlative	37
	Adjectives formed from place names	38
	Adjectives used as nouns	38
	Possessive adjectives	39
5. **Pronouns**	Personal	40
	Interrogative	40
	Relative	41
	Reflexive	41
	Ein and possessive adjectives as pronouns	42
6. **Adverbs**	Formation	43
	Order	43
	Comparative and superlative	43
7. **Prepositions**	Governing the accusative	45
	Governing the genitive	45
	Governing the dative	45
	Governing accusative or dative	46
	Common constructions with prepositions	46
8. **Miscella-neous**	Indirect speech and question	56
	Conditional sentences	57
	Word order — verbs	58
	nicht	58
	adverbs	58
	objects	59
	conjunctions	59
	Numerals — cardinal numbers	60
	ordinal numbers	60
	fractions	61
	Time	61
	Dates	62
	Weak masculine nouns	63
	Nouns in apposition	64

Cases

Nominative

Used (a) for the subject of a sentence

e.g. **Der Vater* ist groß†, die Mutter ist klein, das Kind ist sehr klein**

(b) after **sein, werden, bleiben, heißen** (the complement)

e.g. **Der Vater ist ein Mann, die Mutter ist eine Frau, und das Kind ist ein Mädchen**

Er wurde ein berühmter Arzt und blieb mein treuer Freund

Accusative

Used (a) for the direct object

e.g. **Der Vater putzt den Wagen, die Mutter hält eine Blume, und das Kind liest ein Buch**

(b) to show duration of time

e.g. **Die Sonne scheint den ganzen Tag** (all day)

Er arbeitete eine Stunde (for an hour)

(c) to show distance covered

e.g. **Er läuft eine Meile** (for a mile)

Das Brett war nur einen Fuß breit (only a foot wide)

(d) to show definite time

e.g. **Jeden Samstag spielt er Fußball** (every Saturday)

Letztes Jahr fuhr er nach Deutschland (last year)

(e) with certain prepositions (see pp 45—6)

e.g. **Die Familie sitzt um den Tisch**

Er lief die Straße entlang

(f) to show direction up or down

e.g. **Er steigt den steilen Weg hinauf** (up the steep path)

Er rutscht die Treppe hinunter (down the steps)

---

*N.B. All nouns in German have capital letters.

†N.B. The German **ß**(ss) symbol is used
  (i) at the end of a word, e.g. **muß, Schluß**
  (ii) before a third consonant, e.g. **mußte, Schloßpark**
  (iii) between two vowels when the first one is long, e.g. **schließen, etwas Großes**

Genitive

(See N.B. i, below)

Used (a) to show possession

e.g. **Der Wagen des Vaters ist blau, die Blume der Mutter ist rot, und das Buch des Kindes ist grün**

(b) to show indefinite time

e.g. **Eines Tages besuchte er seine Tante** (one day)
Eines Morgens stand er früh auf (one morning)

(c) with certain prepositions (see p 45)

e.g. **Trotz des Wetters geht er spazieren**
Der Bauernhof liegt unweit des Dorfes

Dative

(See N.B. ii, below)

Used (a) for the indirect object

e.g. **Der Vater gibt dem Kind eine Puppe**
Er schreibt seiner Mutter einen Brief

(b) with certain prepositions (see pp 45—6)

e.g. **Er kommt aus dem Haus**
Er wohnt der Kirche gegenüber

(c) to show possession (normally parts of the body only)
(See also reflexive verbs p 27)

e.g. **Ich wasche mir das Gesicht**
Er klopft seinem Freund auf die Schulter

(d) with certain verbs (see p 29)

e.g. **Der Hund folgt der Katze**
Ich helfe meiner Mutter beim Abwaschen

N.B. (i) Masculine and neuter nouns add **-s** or **-es** in the genitive singular

e.g. **Der Wagen des Vaters**
In der Mitte des Marktplatzes
Die Bücher des Kindes

(ii) All nouns in the dative plural must end in **-n** except those forming their plural with **-s**

e.g. **Die Kinder sind in den Zimmern**
In den Flugzeugen sind 36 Sitzplätze
Die Kinder spielen in den Parks

(iii) Nouns and pronouns in apposition must be in the same case (see p 64)

e.g. **Hier ist mein Bruder, der Fußballspieler**
    Kennst du meinen Bruder, den Fußballspieler?
    Hier ist ein Bild meines Bruders, des Fußballspielers
    Ich sprach mit meinem Bruder, dem Fußballspieler

Articles

The definite article (the)

	M.	F.	N.	Pl.
N.	der	die	das	die
A.	den	die	das	die
G.	des	der	des	der
D.	dem	der	dem	den

The indefinite article (a, an)

	M.	F.	N.
N.	ein	eine	ein
A.	einen	eine	ein
G.	eines	einer	eines
D.	einem	einer	einem

The negative article (not a, no, not any)

nicht ein = kein

	M.	F.	N.	Pl.
N.	kein	keine	kein	keine
A.	keinen	keine	kein	keine
G.	keines	keiner	keines	keiner
D.	keinem	keiner	keinem	keinen

Demonstrative adjectives

(a) *Stems*

dies- this   manch- many a, many
jed- each, every   solch- such
jen- that   welch- which

(b) *Endings*

	M.	F.	N.	Pl.
N.	**-ER**	**-E**	**-ES**	**-E**
A.	**-EN**	**-E**	**-ES**	**-E**
G.	**-ES**	**-ER**	**-ES**	**-ER**
D.	**-EM**	**-ER**	**-EM**	**-EN**

e.g. **Dieses Mädchen wohnt in jenem Haus.**

Derselbe (the same)

	M.	F.	N.	Pl.
N.	**derselbe**	**dieselbe**	**dasselbe**	**dieselben**
A.	**denselben**	**dieselbe**	**dasselbe**	**dieselben**
G.	**desselben**	**derselben**	**desselben**	**derselben**
D.	**demselben**	**derselben**	**demselben**	**denselben**

USES OF THE ARTICLES, ETC

Contractions of the definite article

The following are the more common contractions:

an das — ans	in dem — im
an dem — am	um das — ums
auf das — aufs	von dem — vom
bei dem — beim	zu dem — zum
in das — ins	zu der — zur

The contracted form is used when we do not wish to stress the definite article. It should be used in the following cases:

am Tag by day
am Sonntag usw on Sunday etc.
im allgemeinen generally
im Gegenteil on the contrary
im Sommer usw in summer etc.
im Juli usw in July etc.
zum Beispiel for example
er hat Sie zum besten he is pulling your leg

9

Special uses of the definite article

(i)   Often before abstract nouns or nouns used in a generalised sense

e.g. **Die Natur** nature   **Das Schicksal** fate
Der Mensch ist sterblich Man is mortal
Das Eisen ist ein Metall Iron is a metal

(ii)   Instead of the possessive adjective with parts of the body or with clothing when it is clear to whom they belong

e.g. **Er steckte die Hand in die Tasche.   Ich wasche mir das Gesicht**

(iii)   Before the names of countries if they are feminine or plural

e.g. **Die Schweiz.   Die Vereinigten Staaten**

(iv)   Before the names of rivers or mountains

e.g. **Die Mosel.   Der Taunus.   Köln liegt am Rhein.
Die Jungfrau ist ein berühmter Berg**

(v)   Where English omits the article with days, months, seasons and meals after a preposition

e.g. **Am Montag** on Monday   **Im Frühling** in Spring
Im August in August   **Nach dem Mittagessen** after
                                 lunch

(vi)   With proper nouns preceded by an adjective

e.g. **Der kleine Hans.   Das heutige Deutschland**

(vii)   Before names of streets etc.

e.g. **Meine Freunde haben eine Wohnung in der Sallstraße
Das Theater liegt am Deinhardplatz**

(viii)   Where English uses the indefinite article in expressions of price, quantity etc.

e.g. **Die Trauben kosten eine Mark das Pfund** (one mark a pound)

(ix)   In certain stock phrases
ins Ausland, im Ausland abroad
in der Schule in school
in der Stadt in town
im Bett in bed
aus dem Bett out of bed
in der Tat in fact
zum Beispiel for example
mit der Bahn usw by train etc.
in die Schule, Kirche gehen to go to school, church

10

Omission of the indefinite article

(i)   After **sein, werden, bleiben** and **heißen** before nouns denoting a profession or nationality, unless there is a defining adjective

e.g. **Er ist Arzt** He is a doctor.

    Er ist ein guter Arzt He is a good doctor.

(ii) In certain stock phrases

e.g. **Er hat guten Appetit** He has a good appetite.

    Er hat Fieber He has a temperature.

    Er hat Kopfschmerzen He has a headache.

    Wir haben Besuch We have a visitor.

    Er hat Eile He is in a hurry.

    Mit leiser (lauter) Stimme In a quiet (loud) voice.

    Es ist schade It's a pity.

    Zu Ende kommen To come to an end.

Some, Any (singular)

There is no equivalent of the French partitive article

e.g. **Ich habe Brot** I have some bread.

    Ich habe keine Milch I have no milk.

Verbs

Persons

	Singular	Plural
First	ich I	wir we
Second familiar	du you	ihr you
Third masculine	er he, it	
feminine	sie she, it	sie they
neuter	es it	
Second polite	Sie you	Sie you

The familiar form is used

(a) among relatives, e.g. **Er fragt seinen Vater: ,,Hast du mein Buch?"**

(b) among close friends, e.g. **Er sagt seinem alten Freund: ,,Du siehst krank aus."**

(c) among children, e.g. **Karl fragt Peter: ,,Siehst du den roten Wagen?"**

(d) by an adult talking to children, e.g. **Der Lehrer sagt: ,,Ihr seid artige Kinder."**

TENSES (indicative)

Present (e.g. **spielen** to play)

Formed by adding the following endings to the verb stem (**spiel-**).

Singular			Plural		
ich	-E	(spiele)	wir	-EN	(spielen)
du	-ST	(spielst)	ihr	-T	(spielt)
er, sie, es	-T	(spielt)	sie	-EN	(spielen)
Sie	-EN	(spielen)	Sie	-EN	(spielen)

N.B. (i) Some strong verbs change their stem vowel in the second familiar and third persons singular (see pp 17-21), e.g. **tragen: du trägst, geben: er gibt.**

(ii) Verbs with stems ending in **-d, -t, chn, -ckn, -dn, -fn, -gn** or **-tn** retain the -e of the first person singular throughout, e.g. **du arbeitest, er öffnet.**

Imperfect

Weak verbs (e.g. **spielen**)

Add the following endings to the stem (**spiel-**).

Singular			Plural		
ich	-TE	(spielte)	wir	-TEN	(spielten)
du	-TEST	(spieltest)	ihr	-TET	(spieltet)
er, sie, es	-TE	(spielte)	sie	-TEN	(spielten)
Sie	-TEN	(spielten)	Sie	-TEN	(spielten)

Strong verbs (e.g. **geben** to give)

(a) *Stem.* Strong verbs change their stem vowel and sometimes the whole stem. These new forms must be learned (see pp 17–21).

(b) *Endings.* Add the following endings to this new stem (**gab-**).

Singular			Plural		
ich		(gab)	wir	-EN	(gaben)
du	-ST	(gabst)	ihr	-T	(gabt)
er, sie, es		(gab)	sie	-EN	(gaben)
Sie	-EN	(gaben)	Sie	-EN	(gaben)

Perfect

(a) *Formation*

Formed by using the present tense of **haben** or **sein** and the past participle

N.B. This past participle goes to the end of the clause (see p 58)

(b) *Haben or sein?*

Haben is used

(i) with all transitive verbs,

e.g. **Ich habe den Mann gesehen. Er hat das Buch gekauft**

(ii) with intransitive verbs which do not show a change of state or place,

e.g. **Es hat heute geregnet. Die Sonne hat den ganzen Tag geschienen**

Sein is used with intransitive verbs showing a change of place (e.g. **gehen**) or state (e.g. **einschlafen**),

e.g. **Er ist in die Stadt gegangen. Ich bin um 4 Uhr eingeschlafen**

(c) *The past participle*

(i) *Weak verbs.* Add **ge-** to the front of the stem and **-(e)t** to the end

e.g. **machen—gemacht   spielen—gespielt   baden—gebadet
atmen—geatmet**

(ii) *Strong verbs.* Like the imperfect stems these must be learned (see pp 17—21)

(iii) *Compound verbs* (see p 26). If the prefix is separable add it to the full past participle of the verb

e.g. **aufgehen—aufgegangen   untergehen—untergegangen**

If the prefix is inseparable there is no **ge-**

e.g. **besprechen—besprochen   empfehlen—empfohlen**

(iv) *Verbs ending in -ieren*

These verbs have no **ge-** in the past participle

e.g. **probieren—probiert   reparieren—repariert**

(v) *Modal verbs*

See page 25, note iv

N.B. The following verbs which take **sein**

abbiegen to turn off (from a road)	**Er ist vom Wege abgebogen**
aufbrechen to set out	**Wir sind um 4 Uhr aufgebrochen**
aufstehen to stand, get up	**Ich bin um 7 Uhr aufgestanden**
aufwachen to wake up	**Er ist um 3 Uhr aufgewacht**
begegnen to meet (see p 29)	**Er ist dem Mann begegnet**
bleiben to stay	**Du bist zu Hause geblieben**
einfallen to occur to (see p 29)	**Es ist mir eingefallen, daß . . .**
folgen to follow (see p 29)	**Der Hund ist seinem Herrn gefolgt**
gelingen to succeed (see p 29)	**Es ist mir gelungen, das Rätsel zu lösen**
geschehen to happen	**Ein Unfall ist geschehen**
kentern to capsize	**Das Boot ist gekentert**
klettern to climb (intrans.)	**Wir sind auf die Berge geklettert**
passieren to happen	**Nichts Wichtiges ist passiert**
reisen to travel	**Er ist nach Deutschland gereist**

sein to be (see pp 15, 16)	**Ich bin in Deutschland gewesen**
stürzen to rush, fall	**Er ist aus dem Haus gestürzt**
umziehen to move (house)	**Die Familie ist neulich umgezogen**
verreisen to go away	**Er ist auf zwei Tage verreist**
verunglücken to have an accident	**Er ist tödlich verunglückt**
vorkommen to happen	**Das ist nur selten vorgekommen**

The pluperfect

Formed by using the imperfect of **haben** or **sein** and the past participle
e.g. **Ich hatte den Mann gesehen.   Er war in die Stadt gegangen**

Future

Formed by using the present tense of **werden** (see p 16) and the infinitive. N.B. (see p 58) This infinitive goes to the end of the clause
e.g. **Ich werde in die Stadt gehen. Du wirst ein Buch kaufen.**

If the future idea is contained elsewhere in the clause, the present not the future tense is normally used
e.g. **Nächstes Jahr fahre ich nach Deutschland**

SEIN, HABEN AND WERDEN

Indicative

	Present	Imperfect	Perfect	Pluperfect
Sein				
ich	bin	war	ist gewesen	war gewesen
du	bist	warst	etc.	etc.
er, sie, es	ist	war		
wir	sind	waren		
ihr	seid	wart		
sie, Sie	sind	waren		

	Present	*Imperfect*	*Perfect*	*Pluperfect*
Haben				
ich	habe	hatte	habe gehabt	hatte gehabt
du	hast	hattest	etc.	etc.
er, sie, es	hat	hatte		
wir	haben	hatten		
ihr	habt	hattet		
sie, Sie	haben	hatten		

	Present	*Imperfect*	*Perfect*	*Pluperfect*
Werden				
ich	werde	wurde	bin geworden	war geworden
du	wirst	wurdest	etc.	etc.
er, sie, es	wird	wurde		
wir	werden	wurden		
ihr	werdet	wurdet		
sie, Sie	werden	wurden		

Subjunctive

	Present	*Imperfect*	*Perfect*	*Pluperfect*
Sein				
ich	sei	wäre	sei gewesen	wäre gewesen
du	seiest	wärest	etc.	etc.
er, sie, es	sei	wäre		
wir	seien	wären		
ihr	seiet	wäret		
sie, Sie	seien	wären		

	Present	*Imperfect*	*Perfect*	*Pluperfect*
Haben				
ich	habe	hätte	habe gehabt	hätte gehabt
du	habest	hättest	etc.	etc
er, sie, es	habe	hätte		
wir	haben	hätten		
ihr	habet	hättet		
sie, Sie	haben	hätten		

	Present	Imperfect	Perfect	Pluperfect
Werden				
ich	werde	würde	**sei geworden**	**wäre geworden**
du	werdest	würdest	etc.	etc.
er, sie, es	werde	würde		
wir	werden	würden		
ihr	werdet	würdet		
sie, Sie	werden	würden		

Strong and irregular weak verbs

N.B. This list is not complete but contains most of the common verbs.

Infinitive	3rd pers. Present	3rd pers. Imperfect	3rd pers. Perfect	Meaning
backen	**bäckt**	**buk**	**hat gebacken**	to bake
befehlen	**befiehlt**	**befahl**	**hat befohlen**	order
beginnen	**beginnt**	**begann**	**hat begonnen**	begin
bergen	**birgt**	**barg**	**hat geborgen**	shelter
beißen	**beißt**	**biß**	**hat gebissen**	bite
biegen	**biegt**	**bog**	**hat gebogen**	bend, turn
bieten	**bietet**	**bot**	**hat geboten**	offer
binden	**bindet**	**band**	**hat gebunden**	tie
bitten	**bittet**	**bat**	**hat gebeten**	ask
blasen	**bläst**	**blies**	**hat geblasen**	blow
bleiben	**bleibt**	**blieb**	**ist geblieben**	stay
braten	**brät**	**briet**	**hat gebraten**	roast
brechen	**bricht**	**brach**	**hat gebrochen**	break (transitive)
			ist gebrochen	break (intr)
brennen	**brennt**	**brannte**	**hat gebrannt**	burn
bringen	**bringt**	**brachte**	**hat gebracht**	bring
denken	**denkt**	**dachte**	**hat gedacht**	think
empfehlen	**empfiehlt**	**empfahl**	**hat empfohlen**	recommend
erschrecken	**erschrickt**	**erschrak**	**ist erschrocken**	be frightened

17

essen	ißt	aß	hat gegessen	eat
fahren	fährt	fuhr	ist gefahren	go (by vehicle) (intr)
			hat gefahren	drive (transitive)
fallen	fällt	fiel	ist gefallen	fall
fangen	fängt	fing	hat gefangen	catch
finden	findet	fand	hat gefunden	find
fliegen	fliegt	flog	ist geflogen	fly
fliehen	flieht	floh	ist geflohen	flee
fließen	fließt	floß	ist geflossen	flow
fressen	frißt	fraß	hat gefressen	eat (of animals)
frieren	friert	fror	hat gefroren	freeze, be cold
geben	gibt	gab	hat gegeben	give
gehen	geht	ging	ist gegangen	go, walk
gelingen	gelingt	gelang	ist gelungen	succeed
gelten	gilt	galt	hat gegolten	be valid, worth
genießen	genießt	genoß	hat genossen	enjoy
geschehen	geschieht	geschah	ist geschehen	happen
gewinnen	gewinnt	gewann	hat gewonnen	win
gießen	gießt	goß	hat gegossen	pour
gleiten	gleitet	glitt	ist geglitten	slide
graben	gräbt	grub	hat gegraben	dig
greifen	greift	griff	hat gegriffen	seize
haben	hat	hatte	hat gehabt	have
halten	hält	hielt	hat gehalten	hold, stop (intr)
hängen	hängt	hing	hat gehangen	hang (intr)
heben	hebt	hob	hat gehoben	raise
heißen	heißt	hieß	hat geheißen	be called
helfen	hilft	half	hat geholfen	help
kennen	kennt	kannte	hat gekannt	know (people, places)

18

klingen	klingt	klang	hat geklungen	sound
kommen	kommt	kam	ist gekommen	come
kriechen	kriecht	kroch	ist gekrochen	creep
laden	lädt	lud	hat geladen	load
lassen	läßt	ließ	hat gelassen	leave
laufen	läuft	lief	ist gelaufen	run
leiden	leidet	litt	hat gelitten	suffer
leihen	leiht	lieh	hat geliehen	lend
lesen	liest	las	hat gelesen	read
liegen	liegt	lag	hat gelegen	lie
lügen	lügt	log	hat gelogen	tell lies
messen	mißt	maß	hat gemessen	measure
nehmen	nimmt	nahm	hat genommen	take
nennen	nennt	nannte	hat genannt	name
pfeifen	pfeift	pfiff	hat gepfiffen	whistle
preisen	preist	pries	hat gepriesen	praise
raten	rät	riet	hat geraten	advise, guess
reiben	reibt	rieb	hat gerieben	rub
reißen	reißt	riß	hat gerissen	tear
reiten	reitet	ritt	ist geritten	ride (horse, etc.) (intr)
			hat geritten	ride (transitive)
rennen	rennt	rannte	ist gerannt	run
riechen	riecht	roch	hat gerochen	smell
rinnen	rinnt	rann	ist geronnen	flow, trickle
rufen	ruft	rief	hat gerufen	call, shout
saugen	saugt	sog	hat gesogen	suck
schaffen	schafft	schuf	hat geschaffen	create
scheinen	scheint	schien	hat geschienen	seem, shine
schelten	schilt	schalt	hat gescholten	blame, scold
schieben	schiebt	schob	hat geschoben	push
schießen	schießt	schoß	hat geschossen	shoot
schlafen	schläft	schlief	hat geschlafen	sleep
schlagen	schlägt	schlug	hat geschlagen	hit
schleichen	schleicht	schlich	ist geschlichen	creep

19

schließen	schließt	schloß	hat geschlossen	
				shut
schmeißen	schmeißt	schmiß	hat geschmissen	
				fling
schmelzen	schmilzt	schmolz	hat geschmolzen	
				melt (trans)
			ist geschmolzen	
				melt (intr)
schneiden	schneidet	schnitt	hat geschnitten	
				cut
schreiben	schreibt	schrieb	hat geschrieben	
				write
schreien	schreit	schrie	hat geschrie(e)n	
				shout, scream
schreiten	schreitet	schritt	ist geschritten	
				stride
schweigen	schweigt	schwieg	hat geschwiegen	
				say nothing
schwimmen	schwimmt	schwamm	hat geschwommen	
				swim
schwingen	schwingt	schwang	hat geschwungen	
				swing
schwören	schwört	schwur	hat geschworen	
				swear, vow
sehen	sieht	sah	hat gesehen	see
sein	ist	war	ist gewesen	be
senden	sendet	sandte	hat gesandt	send
		sendete	hat gesendet	
singen	singt	sang	hat gesungen	sing
sinken	sinkt	sank	ist gesunken	sink (intr)
sitzen	sitzt	saß	hat gesessen	be sitting
speien	speit	spie	hat gespie(e)n	spit
sprechen	spricht	sprach	hat gesprochen	
				speak
springen	springt	sprang	ist gesprungen	jump
stechen	sticht	stach	hat gestochen	prick, sting
stehen	steht	stand	hat gestanden	stand

20

stehlen	stiehlt	stahl	hat gestohlen	steal
steigen	steigt	stieg	ist gestiegen	climb
sterben	stirbt	starb	ist gestorben	die
stoßen	stößt	stieß	hat gestoßen	push
streiten	streitet	stritt	hat gestritten	argue
tragen	trägt	trug	hat getragen	carry, wear
treffen	trifft	traf	hat getroffen	meet, hit
treiben	treibt	trieb	hat getrieben	drive, go in for
treten	tritt	trat	ist getreten	tread, step
trinken	trinkt	trank	hat getrunken	drink
tun	tut	tat	hat getan	do
verderben	verdirbt	verdarb	hat verdorben	spoil
vergessen	vergißt	vergaß	hat vergessen	forget
verlieren	verliert	verlor	hat verloren	lose
vermeiden	vermeidet	vermied	hat vermieden	avoid
ver-schwinden	ver-schwindet	ver-schwand	ist verschwunden	disappear
verzeihen	verzeiht	verzieh	hat verziehen	pardon
wachsen	wächst	wuchs	ist gewachsen	grow
waschen	wäscht	wusch	hat gewaschen	wash
weisen	weist	wies	hat gewiesen	point, show
wenden	wendet	wandte	hat gewandt	turn (trans.)
		wendete	hat gewendet	
werden	wird	wurde	ist geworden	become
werfen	wirft	warf	hat geworfen	throw
wiegen	wiegt	wog	hat gewogen	weigh (intr)
winden	windet	wand	hat gewunden	twist, wind
wissen*	weiß	wußte	hat gewußt	know (facts)
ziehen	zieht	zog	hat gezogen	pull
			ist gezogen	go, move
zwingen	zwingt	zwang	hat gezwungen	force

*wissen present tense: ich weiß, du weißt, er weiß, wir wissen, ihr wißt, sie wissen.

SUBJUNCTIVE

Present tense (e.g. spielen)

Formed by adding the following endings to the stem (**spiel-**).

Singular			Plural		
ich	-E	(spiele)	wir	-EN	(spielen)
du	-EST	(spielest)	ihr	-ET	(spielet)
er, sie, es	-E	(spiele)	sie	-EN	(spielen)
Sie	-EN	(spielen)	Sie	-EN	(spielen)

N.B. Strong verbs do not change their stem vowel.
e.g. **Er gebe, du sprechest**

Imperfect tense

(i) *Weak verbs* (e.g. **spielen**)

Add the following endings to the stem.

Singular			Plural		
ich	-TE	(spielte)	wir	-TEN	(spielten)
du	-TEST	(spieltest)	ihr	-TET	(spieltet)
er, sie, es	-TE	(spielte)	sie	-TEN	(spielten)
Sie	-TEN	(spielten)	Sie	-TEN	(spielten)

N.B. This is the same as the imperfect indicative.

(ii) *Strong verbs* (e.g. **geben**)

Formed by adding the following endings to the 3rd person singular imperfect indicative and by adding an umlaut to the stem vowel (**gäb-**).

Singular			Plural		
ich	-E	(gäbe)	wir	-EN	(gäben)
du	-EST	(gäbest)	ihr	-ET	(gäbet)
er, sie, es	-E	(gäbe)	sie	-EN	(gäben)
Sie	-EN	(gäben)	Sie	-EN	(gäben)

Perfect and pluperfect

Formed in the same way as the indicative except that the subjunctive forms of the auxiliary verbs are used (see pp 16, 17)
e.g. **Er sei in die Stadt gegangen**
     Er hätte Fußball gespielt

Future

Formed in the same way as the indicative except that the present subjunctive of **werden** is used (see p 17)

e.g. **Du werdest in die Stadt gehen**
    Er werde Fußball spielen

Modals

Form their subjunctives like regular weak verbs.

e.g. **Du solltest in die Stadt gehen**
    Er könnte Fußball spielen

Uses of the subjunctive

(i)   In indirect speech and question (see p 56)
(ii) In some conditional clauses (see p 57)
(iii) After **als ob** (as if).
(iv) In exclamatory wishes, e.g. **Lang lebe die Königin!**
(v) Sometimes after the conjunction **damit** in the past,
e.g. **Er stand auf, damit wir ihn sehen könnten.**

MODAL VERBS

	Dürfen to be allowed to	**Können** to be able to	**Mögen** to like, want to
Present Indic.			
ich	darf	kann	mag
du	darfst	kannst	magst
er, sie, es	darf	kann	mag
wir	dürfen	können	mögen
ihr	dürft	könnt	mögt
sie, Sie	dürfen	können	mögen
Present Subjunc.			
ich	dürfe	könne	möge

23

Imperfect Indic.

ich	**durfte**	**konnte**	**mochte**

Imp. Subjunc.

ich	**dürfte**	**könnte**	**möchte**

Perfect Indic.

ich habe	(i) **gedurft**	(i) **gekonnt**	(i) **gemocht**
	(ii) **dürfen***	(ii) **können***	(ii) **mögen***

Future Indic.

ich werde	**dürfen**	**können**	**mögen**

	Müssen	**Sollen**	**Wollen**	**Lassen†**
	to have to	to ought to	to want to	to let, allow

Present Indic.

ich	**muß**	**soll**	**will**	**lasse**
du	**mußt**	**sollst**	**willst**	**läßt**
er, sie, es	**muß**	**soll**	**will**	**läßt**
wir	**müssen**	**sollen**	**wollen**	**lassen**
ihr	**müßt**	**sollt**	**wollt**	**laßt**
sie, Sie	**müssen**	**sollen**	**wollen**	**lassen**

Present Subjunc.

ich	**müsse**	**solle**	**wolle**	**lasse**

Imperfect Indic.

ich	**mußte**	**sollte**	**wollte**	**ließ**

Imp. Subjunc.

ich	**müßte**	**sollte**	**wollte**	**ließe**

Perfect Indic.

ich habe	(i) **ge-mußt**	(i) **ge-sollt**	(i) **ge-wollt**	(i) **ge-lassen**
	(ii) **müs-sen***	(ii) **sol-len***	(ii) **wol-len***	(ii) **lassen***

Future Indic.

ich werde	**müssen**	**sollen**	**wollen**	**lassen**

*see note iv   †not a modal but behaves like one.

24

Notes on modal verbs

(i) These verbs are irregular in the singular of the present tense.

(ii) They are followed by a plain infinitive, i.e. no **zu** (see p 30)

e.g. **Ich muß diese Verben lernen**

(iii) There is no umlaut in the imperfect indicative of **dürfen, können, mögen, müssen.**

(iv) After the infinitive of another verb the infinitive and not the past participle is used in the perfect and pluperfect tenses.

e.g. **Er hat es gemocht** but **Er hat es tun mögen**

Er hat es gewollt but **Er hat das Buch lesen wollen**

(v) The subjunctive forms follow the weak verb pattern (see p 22).

Some uses of modal verbs

Dürfen

Er durfte alles machen He was allowed to do anything

Es dürfte wahr sein It may be true

Können

Es kann sein It may be

Es kann vielleicht regnen It may rain

Er kann Deutsch He knows German

Ich kann nichts dafür I can't help it

Er kann es unmöglich tragen He can't possibly carry it

Ich kann es getan haben I may have done it

Ich habe es tun können I was able to do it

Mögen

Er mag kommen He may come

Das mag wohl sein That may be

Es mag wohl zehn Tage her sein It must be about ten days ago

Er mag zwei Jahre alt gewesen sein He may have been two years old

Ich möchte Deutschland besuchen I should like to visit Germany

Müssen

Ich mußte es tun I had to do it

Er muß es getan haben He must have done it

Er hat es tun müssen He has had to do it

Sollen

Was soll das? What does that mean?
Er soll reich sein He is supposed (said) to be rich
Der Kranke soll zu Bett gehen The sick man is to go to bed
Der Wagen sollte uns zum Bahnhof bringen The car was to take us to the station
Was sollte ich anfangen? What was I to do?
Er sollte (subjunc) **es tun** He ought to do it
Er hätte es tun sollen He ought to have done it
Er soll es getan haben He is supposed (said) to have done it

Wollen

Wollen Sie mitkommen? Do you want to come with us?
Wir wollen ins Kino gehen! Let's go to the pictures (see p 31)
Ich will eben ausgehen I am just going out
Ich wollte eben ausgehen I was just going out

Lassen

Ich ließ es dort liegen I left it lying there
Laß uns gehen! Let's go (see p 31)
Er hat mich warten lassen He made me wait
Er ließ sich ein Haus bauen He had a house built
Das läßt sich nicht leugnen That can't be denied
Er hat den Arzt kommen lassen He sent for the doctor
Er läßt Sie grüßen He sends his best wishes
Laß dich nicht stören Don't let me disturb you

COMPOUND VERBS

Inseparable prefixes

Verbs compounded with the following prefixes are inseparable.

| be- | ent- | ge- | ver- |
| emp- | er- | miß - | zer- |

Separable or inseparable prefixes

The following prefixes may be separable or inseparable:

| durch- | über- | unter- | wider- |
| hinter- | um- | voll- | wieder- |

They are usually separable if the verb can be translated literally
e.g. **übersetzen: Er setzte mich über** He ferried me across.

        Er übersetzte das Buch He translated the book.

Separable prefixes

All other prefixes are separable.

N.B. (i) The separable prefix goes to the end of the clause except when the infinitive or past participle is used and in subordinate clauses.

(ii) When the infinitive is used with **zu** the **zu** is put between the prefix and the verb. E.g. **er versuchte, auszusteigen.**

(iii) **ge-** is retained in the past participle (see p 14)

REFLEXIVE VERBS

There are two types of reflexive verbs. In one the pronoun is the direct object and so accusative; in the other it is a dative of possession.

Accusative	*Dative*
ich wasche mich	ich wasche mir die Hände
du wäschst dich	du wäschst dir die Hände
er, sie, es wäscht sich	er, sie, es wäscht sich die Hände
wir waschen uns	wir waschen uns die Hände
ihr wascht euch	ihr wascht euch die Hände
sie waschen sich	sie waschen sich die Hände
Sie waschen sich	Sie waschen sich die Hände

N.B. (i) The reflexive pronoun follows the subject as closely as possible.

e.g. **Ich muß mir die Hände vor dem Mittagessen waschen.**

(ii) **Er wäscht seine Hände:** The hands do not belong to the subject.

THE PASSIVE

Formation

The passive is formed by using the appropriate tense of **werden** (see pp 16—17) plus the past participle of the verb to be put in the passive.

N.B. (i) This past participle goes to the end of the clause.

(ii) When the perfect or pluperfect of **werden** is used, **worden** not **geworden** is used and follows the other past participle.

By

The English word "by" is expressed

(a) by **von** when it refers to the agent or agency, e.g. **Der Ball wurde von dem Jungen geschlagen, Der Baum wurde vom Sturm umrissen.**

(b) by **durch** to express means, e.g. **Er wurde von seiner Mutter durch ein heftiges Schütteln geweckt.**

(c) by **mit** to express the instrument, e.g. **Der Brief war mit einer Feder geschrieben worden.**

The infinitive

The passive infinitive is formed by using the past participle of the verb plus **werden**, e.g. **Er konnte von allen gehört werden.**
Sometimes by **sein** + **zu** + the infinitive, e.g. **Niemand war zu sehen.**

Avoidance of the passive

(a) by using a reflexive verb, e.g. **Die Tür öffnete sich.**
(b) by using **man** with an active verb, e.g. **Man öffnete die Tür.**

THE CONDITIONAL

Formation

Formed by using the imperfect subjunctive of **werden** (see p 17) plus the infinitive of the verb.

Uses

(a) Used of an action that was to take place at some future time
e.g. **Ich wußte, daß er kommen würde.**
(b) In some conditional sentences (see p 57)
e.g. **Ich würde es machen, wenn ich Zeit hätte.**

The conditional perfect

This is usually replaced by the pluperfect subjunctive
e.g. **Ich hätte es getan** rather than **Ich würde es getan haben.**

IMPERSONAL VERBS

The following verbs are used impersonally.

(N.B. the use of the dative with most of them.)

einfallen to occur to. e.g. **Es fällt mir ein.**

fehlen (an + dative) to lack (something). e.g. **Es fehlt mir an Büchern.**

freuen to be glad. e.g. **Es freut mich, daß ...**

gefallen to please, **mißfallen** to displease. e.g. **Es gefällt mir** (I like).

gelingen to succeed, **mißlingen** to fail. e.g. **Es gelingt mir** (I manage, succeed).

N.B. the following phrases using verbs impersonally.

Was fehlt dir? What's the matter with you?

Es geht mir gut I am well

Wie geht's dir How are you?

Mir ist, als ob I feel as if

Es ist mir warm (kalt) I am warm (cold)

Es schadet nichts It doesn't matter

Es tut mir leid I am sorry

Es tut mir weh It hurts me

VERBS GOVERNING THE DATIVE

antworten to answer (someone)

befehlen to command

begegnen to meet

danken to thank

dienen to serve

drohen to threaten

einfallen to occur to (see above)

entgehen } to escape from
entkommen

erlauben to allow

folgen to follow

gefallen to please (see above)

gehorchen to obey

gehören to belong to

gelingen to succeed (see above)

gleichen to resemble, look like

gratulieren to congratulate

glauben to believe (someone)

helfen to help

leid tun um to be sorry for (see above)

mißfallen to displease (see above)

passen to suit

raten to advise

trauen to trust

verzeihen to forgive

29

weh tun to hurt (see p 29)   **zuhören** to listen to
widersprechen to contradict   **zusehen** to watch

e.g. **Seine Mutter hilft ihm bei den Schulaufgaben.**
     Ich bin ihm begegnet.

N.B. This is not a complete list but contains most of the common verbs.

THE DEPENDENT INFINITIVE WITH AND WITHOUT *ZU*

Modal verbs (see p 23)

Zu is not required before the infinitive after a modal verb
e.g. **Ich kann diese Aufgaben leicht machen.**
     Er wollte in die Stadt gehen.

Lassen, bleiben, fühlen, hören, sehen

Zu is not required before an infinitive used with these verbs
e.g. **Ich ließ den Hund weglaufen**
     Er läßt sich ein Haus bauen He is having a house built.
     Er blieb da sitzen
     Ich fühlte die Katze schnurren
     Ich sah ihn kommen

Heißen, helfen, lehren, lernen

In short simple sentences or ones in which these verbs follow their
dependent infinitive **zu** is not required
e.g. **Er hieß den Kellner kommen**
     Er lehrt mich schwimmen
     Er half seiner Mutter aufräumen
     Er wird mich schwimmen lehren
     Die Mutter hat die Tochter stricken gelehrt
     Ich habe schwimmen gelernt

In longer sentences or ones in which the dependent infinitive follows
the verb, zu is required
e.g. **Wer hat dich geheißen, hierher zu kommen?**
     Sein Vater hat ihn gelehrt, einen Wagen zu fahren
     Er half mir, den Wagen bis zur Garage zu bringen
     Er hat endlich gelernt, seinen eigenen Namen zu schreiben

30

Other verbs and verbal expressions

After all other verbs and verbal expressions **zu** is needed

e.g. **Er bat mich zu kommen**

   Es ist leicht, das zu sagen

N.B. for the position of **zu** with separable verbs see p 27.

IMPERATIVES

Du form

(a) Add -*e* to the verb stem

e.g. **laufen — laufe!**

N.B. This -*e* is often omitted, especially in direct speech

e.g. **Komm schnell! Trag die Teller in die Küche!**

(b) If the stem vowel changes from **e** to **ie** or **i** drop the -*st* ending from the **du** form present tense.

e.g. **nehmen – du nimmst – nimm!   sehen – du siehst – sieh!**

Ihr form

Use the **ihr** form present tense without the **ihr**

e.g. **geben — ihr gebt — gebt!**

Sie form

Invert the **Sie** form of the present tense

e.g. **geben — Sie geben — geben Sie!**

Wir form

Formed in one of three ways:

(a) Invert the **wir** form present tense

e.g. **gehen — wir gehen — gehen wir!**

(b) Using **wollen**

e.g. **wir wollen gehen!**

(c) Using **lassen**

e.g. **laß (laßt or lassen Sie) uns gehen!**

N.B. All imperatives should be followed by an exclamation mark.

Sein, haben and werden

	Du	Ihr	Sie
Sein	Sei!	Seid!	Seien Sie!
Haben	Habe!	Habt!	Haben Sie!
Werden	Werde!	Werdet!	Werden Sie!

Reflexives

	Du	Ihr	Sie
Accusative	Wasche dich!	Wascht euch!	Waschen Sie sich!
Dative	Wasche dir die Hände!	Wascht euch die Hände!	Waschen Sie sich die Hände!

PRESENT PARTICIPLES

Formation

Formed by adding **-d** to the infinitive
e.g. **kommen—kommend**

Use

Normally used only as adjectives and therefore take the normal adjectival endings (see pp 35—37).
e.g. **ein dauernder Erfolg**
(See also below)

ENGLISH VERBAL FORMS IN -ING

These can be translated in several ways.

(a) By a present participle used adjectively (see above)
e.g. **Die folgende Geschichte** The following story.

(b) By an infinitive used as a noun (N.B. these are always neuter)
e.g. **Ich bin des Stehens müde** I'm tired of standing.

(c) By the simple infinitive after **bleiben, finden, fühlen, hören, lassen** and **sehen**.

e.g. **Ich ließ es dort liegen** I left it lying there.

(d) The infinitive with **zu** when there is no change in the subject.

e.g. after **ohne, anstatt,** etc.

e.g. **Er kam ins Zimmer, ohne mich zu sehen** He came into the room without seeing me.

Es ist leicht, Deutsch zu lernen Learning German is easy.

(e) By a dependent clause, e.g. introduced by **indem** (by -ing), **daß, ohne daß, anstatt daß, da, nachdem, ehe,** etc.

e.g. **Er kam ins Zimmer, ohne daß ich ihn sah** He came into the room without my seeing him.

(f) By a dependent clause introduced by **wie** after verbs of seeing or hearing.

e.g. **Ich hörte, wie er die Treppe hinaufkam** I heard him coming up the stairs.

(g) By a relative clause

e.g. **Der Mann, der die Zeitung las, schlief ein** The man reading the paper fell asleep.

(h) By a main clause introduced by **und**

e.g. **Er schlief fest und wachte um 9 Uhr auf** He slept soundly, waking at 9 o'clock.

(i) The past participle of a verb of motion after **kommen**

e.g. **Er kam auf mich zugelaufen** He came running up to me.

(j) By a finite verb with **gern, lieber, am liebsten**

e.g. **Ich spiele gern Fußball** I like playing football.

(k) By a preposed adjectival clause

e.g. **Die Fußball spielenden Kinder machten viel Lärm** The children playing football made a lot of noise.

(l) Note also the continuous sense of the various tenses

Ich schreibe einen Brief I am writing a letter

Er las die Zeitung He was reading the paper

Er hat dem Fernsehen zugesehen He has been watching television

Ich hatte im Wohnzimmer gearbeitet I had been working in the lounge

TENSES AFTER *SEIT*

Note the differences between the English tenses and the German ones used after **seit.**

(a) **Seit wann lernen Sie Deutsch?** How long have you been learning German?

The Germans use the present tense because you have been and still are learning German.

(b) **Er wohnte seit zwei Jahren in Berlin, als der Krieg begann**
He had been living in Berlin for two years when the war began.

The Germans use the imperfect because he had been and still was living in Berlin.

N.B. The Germans use the same tense as the English if the sentence is negative.

e.g. **Ich habe ihn seit Jahren nicht gesehen** I haven't seen him for years.

Adjectives

Agreement of adjectives

Adjectives used predicatively do not decline
e.g. **Der Mann ist gut — Die Männer sind gut.**
But if an adjective precedes its noun then the appropriate ending must
be added. There are six groups of endings.

(a) *Der* group
After **der, dieser, jener, jeder, solcher, welcher** and **mancher**
(sing.) the following endings are added.

	M.	F.	N.	Pl.
N.	-E	-E	-E	-EN
A.	-EN	-E	-E	-EN
G.	-EN	-EN	-EN	-EN
D.	-EN	-EN	-EN	-EN

e.g. **Der alte Mann hat die neuen Bücher.**
Die junge Frau wohnt in dem neuen Haus.

(b) *Ein* group
After **ein**

	M.	F.	N.	Pl.
N.	-ER	-E	-ES	-E
A.	-EN	-E	-ES	-E
G.	-EN	-EN	-EN	-ER
D.	-EN	-EN	-EN	-EN

e.g. **Neue Bücher liegen auf einem runden Tisch.**

(c) *Kein* group
After **kein** and the possessive adjectives (see p 39).

	M.	F.	N.	Pl.
N.	-ER	-E	-ES	-EN
A.	-EN	-E	-ES	-EN
G.	-EN	-EN	-EN	-EN
D.	-EN	-EN	-EN	-EN

e.g. **Seine junge Tochter hat keine alten Puppen.**

(d) *No defining word*

	M.	F.	N.	Pl.
N.	-ER	-E	-ES	-E
A.	-EN	-E	-ES	-E
G.	-EN	-ER	-EN	-ER
D.	-EM	-ER	-EM	-EN

e.g. **Nach vielen Tagen sonnigen Wetters**

(e) *After* **einige, wenige, ein paar, manche** (*plural*), **viele** *and* **mehrere**.

	Pl.
N.	-E
A.	-E
G.	-ER
D.	-EN

e.g. **Ein paar reiche Leute wohnen in vielen großen Häusern**

(f) *After* ***Alle***

The demonstrative or possessive adjective after **alle** has the same ending as **alle**. Any other adjective takes *-en.*

e.g.
- N. **alle diese (meine) neuen Bücher**
- A. **alle diese (meine) neuen Bücher**
- G. **aller dieser (meiner) neuen Bücher**
- D. **allen diesen (meinen) neuen Büchern**

Adjectives after *nichts* etc.

After **etwas, viel, soviel, wenig, nichts** and **allerlei** the adjective is written with a capital letter* and takes the following endings.

N.	-ES
A.	-ES
G.	-EN
D.	-EM

e.g. **Ich habe nichts Neues gesehen.**

---

* **ander, möglich, übrig** and **einzig** are exceptions and retain the small letter.
e.g. **etwas anderes.**

Adjectives after *alles* etc.

After **alles**, **vieles** and **weniges** the adjective is written with a capital letter* and takes the following endings

N.	**-E**
A.	**-E**
G.	**-EN**
D.	**-EN**

e.g. **Ich wünsche dir alles Gute**

*ander, möglich, übrig and einzig retain the small letter.

THE COMPARATIVE AND SUPERLATIVE

Stems

To form the comparative stem add *-er* to the adjective.
To form the superlative stem add *-(e)st* to the adjective.
N.B. Most monosyllabic adjectives add an umlaut.

e.g.

Positive	*Comparative*	*Superlative*
schnell	**schneller**	**schnellst**
warm	**wärmer**	**wärmst**

Declension

Comparative and superlative adjectives decline like normal adjectives.
(see pp 35—37)
e.g. **ein schnellerer Zug — der schnellste Zug**

Predicative superlative

Add *-(e)sten* to the adjective and put **am** in front.
e.g. **Der Schwarzwald ist im Winter am schönsten. Hier ist der Fluß am breitesten.**

Additional example: **Koblenz ist groß, Köln ist größer, Berlin ist am größten**

Than and as

longer than **länger *als***
not longer than **nicht länger *als***
not so long as **nicht *so* lang *wie***
as long as **(eben) *so* lang *wie***

Irregular adjectives

Positive	Comparative	Superlative
groß	größer	größt
hoch	höher	höchst
viel[1]	mehr[2]	die meisten (pl. only)
gut	besser	best
nah	näher	nächst

[1] does not decline in the singular (except **Vielen Dank**)
[2] does not decline

False superlatives

e.g. He is most clever **Er ist höchst (äußerst) klug.**

Note the following construction
Immer besser better and better   **Immer mehr** more and more
Immer schneller quicker and quicker

ADJECTIVES FORMED FROM PLACE NAMES

Adjectives can be formed from names of cities etc. by adding *-er* to the place name.

N.B. (i) these adjectives have a capital letter.

(ii) they do not decline

e.g. **Der Nürnberger Dom**   **Die Berliner Straßen**

ADJECTIVES USED AS NOUNS

When adjectives are used as nouns they are
(i) *declined* liked ordinary adjectives (see pp 35—37)
(ii) written with a *capital letter*

(*Masculine*)

Singular	Plural	Singular	Plural
der Fremde	die Fremden	ein Fremder	Fremde
den Fremden	die Fremden	einen Fremden	Fremde
des Fremden	der Fremden	eines Fremden	Fremder
dem Fremden	den Fremden	einem Fremden	Fremden

Wohnt die alte Frau hier?   Ja, *die Alte* wohnt hier.
Kennst du den alten Mann?   Ja, ich kenne *den Alten.*
Der Mann der alten Frau ist krank.   Der Mann *der Alten* ist krank.

**Was gibt die alte Frau ihrem kranken Mann? Sie gibt
ihrem Kranken Medizin.**

The most common adjectival nouns are:

der Alte, ein Alter old man
der Beamte, ein Beamter official
der Bekannte, ein Bekannter acquaintance
der Deutsche, ein Deutscher German
der Erwachsene, ein Erwachsener adult
der Fremde, ein Fremder stranger, foreigner
der Reisende, ein Reisender traveller
der Verwandte, ein Verwandter relative

**Der Reisende sprach mit dem Beamten an der Grenze.
Wir besuchten unsere Verwandten in Berlin.
Ich begegnete einem Bekannten in der Stadt.**

POSSESSIVE ADJECTIVES

Stems

ich – **mein**	my		wir – **unser**	our
du – **dein**	your		ihr – **euer**	your
er – **sein**	his, its			
sie – **ihr**	her, its		sie – **ihr**	their
es – **sein**	its			
Sie – **Ihr**	your		Sie – **Ihr**	your

Declension

To these stems are added the following endings

	M.	F.	N.	Pl.
N	-	-E	-	-E
A.	-EN	-E	-	-E
G.	-ES	-ER	-ES	-ER
D.	-EM	-ER	-EM	-EN

N.B. (i) When **euer** has an ending it drops its second **e**
e.g. **Euer Vater** but **das Buch eures Vaters**

(ii) Similarly the **e** may also be omitted from **unser** when it has an
ending.
e.g. **Unsere Bücher** or **unsre Bücher**

Pronouns

Personal pronouns

Nom.	Acc.	Dat.	Nom.	Acc.	Dat.
ich	mich	mir	wir	uns	uns
du	dich	dir	ihr	euch	euch
er	ihn	ihm			
sie	sie	ihr	sie	sie	ihnen
es	es	ihm			
Sie	Sie	Ihnen	Sie	Sie	Ihnen

N.B. (i) If the pronoun refers to a thing or things and is governed by a preposition, **da (dar)** plus the preposition is used instead of the pronoun.

e.g. **mit dem Lehrer — mit ihm**   but **mit dem Bleistift — damit**
auf dem Stuhl — darauf

(ii) 'it' can be masculine or feminine as well as neuter in German depending on the gender of the noun it replaces.

Interrogative pronouns

	Persons	Things
N.	wer	was
A.	wen	was (wo/wor + preposition)
G.	wessen	wessen
D.	wem	wo/wor + preposition.

N.B. If the pronoun refers to a thing or things and is governed by a preposition, **wo(wor)** plus the preposition is used instead of the pronoun (cf. note on personal pronouns).

e.g. **Er geht mit dem Vater spazieren — *mit wem* geht er spazieren?** but **Er schreibt mit dem Bleistift — *womit* schreibt er?**

Relative pronouns

	M.	F.	N.	Pl.
N.	der	die	das	die
A.	den	die	das	die
G.	dessen	deren	dessen	deren
D.	dem	der	dem	denen

N.B. (i) The relative pronoun agrees in number and gender with the noun to which it refers (i.e. its antecedent).

(ii) The case of the pronoun depends on the part it plays in the relative clause.

(iii) The relative pronoun clause immediately follows the antecedent.

(iv) The verb goes to the end of the relative clause.

(v) The relative clause is separated from the rest of the sentence by commas.

(vi) If the pronoun is governed by a preposition and refers to a thing or things, **wo(wor)** plus the preposition may be used instead of the pronoun.

e.g. **Die Frau, deren Sohn krank war, war traurig.**

Das Haus, wovor (or **vor dem**) **ich stehe, ist sehr alt.**

N.B. The relative pronoun cannot be omitted in German as it is in English.

e.g. The book I am reading is interesting. **Das Buch, das ich lese, ist interessant.**

Reflexive pronouns

(Cf. reflexive verbs p 27)

	Acc.	Dat.		Acc.	Dat.
ich	mich	mir	wir	uns	uns
du	dich	dir	ihr	euch	euch
er					
sie	sich	sich	sie	sich	sich
es					
Sie	sich	sich	Sie	sich	sich

e.g. **Er machte die Tür hinter sich zu** He shut the door behind him (self).

Er hat sich das Bein gebrochen He has broken his leg.

Ein and the possessive adjectives used as pronouns

Add the following endings to the stem (see p 39)

	M.	F.	N.	Pl.
N.	-ER	-E	-ES	-E
A.	-EN	-E	-ES	-E
G.	-ES	-ER	-ES	-ER
D.	-EM	-ER	-EM	-EN

N.B. (i) The pronoun thus formed is the same gender as the noun to which it refers.

(ii) Its case depends on the part it plays in the sentence.

e.g. **Dein Bruder ist älter als mein*er*.**
   Sie spricht mit ein*em* meiner Freunde.

N.B. also **der mein(ig)e, die mein(ig)e, das mein(ig)e, die mein(ig)en,** etc.

e.g. **Hier ist mein Buch. Wo is das dein(ig)e?**

Adverbs

Formation

Almost all adjectives can also be used as adverbs, e.g. **die schöne Frau singt schön**.

N.B. The following are common exceptions.

blindlings blindly	**teils** ⎫
(un)glücklicherweise	**teilweise** ⎭ partly
(un)fortunately	**vorwärts** (etc.) forwards
lange for a long time	**wochenlang** (etc.) for weeks
morgens (etc.) in the morning	

Order of adverbs

If two or more adverbs or adverbial phrases occur in a sentence they must come in the following order.

1. TIME   2. MANNER   3. PLACE

e.g. **Jeden Morgen fahre ich mit dem Bus in die Stadt.**

If two adverbs of the same sort occur in a sentence the more general precedes the more specific.

e.g. **Er saß im Garten unter dem Apfelbaum.**

COMPARATIVE AND SUPERLATIVE

Regular adverbs

(i) The comparative is formed by adding *-er* to the positive form.

(ii) The superlative is formed by adding *-(e)sten* to the positive form and putting **am** in front.

(iii) Most adverbs of one syllable take an umlaut in the comparative and superlative.

e.g.

Positive	*Comparative*	*Superlative*
kalt	**kälter**	**am kältesten**
freundlich	**freundlicher**	**am freundlichsten**

43

Irregular adverbs

Positive	Comparative	Superlative
bald	eher	am ehesten
	früher	am frühsten
gern	lieber	am liebsten
gut (wohl)	besser	am besten
oft (häufig)	öfter	am öftesten
	häufiger	am häufigsten
viel (sehr)	mehr	am meisten
wenig	weniger	am wenigsten
	minder	am mindesten

Prepositions

Governing the accusative

ausgenommen except
bis till, to, as far as
durch through, by
entlang along
für for, on behalf of

gegen against, towards, about
ohne without
um round, at
wider against

N.B. **Ausgenommen** and **entlang** follow their nouns.

Governing the genitive

(an)statt instead of
außerhalb outside
diesseits this side of
inmitten among
innerhalb inside
jenseits the other side of
kraft by virtue of
(ver) mittels by means of

trotz in spite of
um ... willen for the sake of
unterhalb below
unweit not far from
während during
wegen because of
zeit during

Governing the dative

aus out of, from
außer except
bei at (Cf. Fr. **chez**)
dank thanks to
entgegen towards
gegenüber opposite

gemäß in accordance with
mit with
nach to, after, according to
seit since, for (time)
von from, of
zu to, at

N.B. (i) **Entgegen** and **gegenüber** normally follow their nouns.

(ii) When **nach** follows its noun it means according to.

Governing the accusative or dative

an on, to, at	**über** over, across, about
auf on to, on	**unter** under, among
hinter behind	**vor** in front of, ago
in in, into	**zwischen** between
neben near, next to	

N.B. (i) They govern the accusative if they show motion to a place.
e.g. **Er geht in das Zimmer.**

(ii) They govern the dative if they show

(a) rest, e.g. **Er ist in dem Zimmer.**

(b) motion at a place, e.g. **Er geht in dem Zimmer auf und ab.**

Some common constructions with prepositions

(i) *An* + *accusative*

Er kommt an die Reihe	it is his turn
Gewohnt an	accustomed to
Denken an	to think of
Sich erinnern an	to remember
Sich gewöhnen an	to get used to

(ii) *An* + *dative*

Er ist an der Reihe } **Die Reihe ist an ihm**	it's his turn
Am Morgen (usw)	in the morning (etc.)
Am nächsten Tag (usw)	on the next day (etc.)
Der Mangel an	the lack of
Der Vorrat an	the supply of
An deiner Stelle	in your place
Nahe an	near
Schuld an	guilty of
Erkennen an	to recognise by
Leiden an	to suffer from
Sich freuen an	to be glad about
Fehlen an	to be lacking in
Teilnehmen an	to take part in
Vorbeigehen (usw) an	to walk (etc.) past

(iii) *Auf* + *accusative*

Auf das Land gehen	to go into the country
Er kam auf mich zu	he came up to me
Er kam auf zwei Tage	he came for two days
Auf diese Weise	in this way
Auf jeden Fall	in any case
Auf deutsch (usw)	in German (etc.)
Die Antwort auf	the answer to
Stolz auf	proud of
Böse auf	angry with
Achten auf ⎫ Aufpassen auf ⎬	to pay attention to
Antworten auf	to answer
Sich freuen auf	to look forward to
Hoffen auf	to hope for
Warten auf	to wait for
Sich verlassen auf	to rely on
Weisen auf ⎫ Zeigen auf ⎬	to point at
Sich auf den Weg machen	to set out

(iv) *Auf* + *dative*

Auf dem Bahnhof	at the station
Auf der Straße	in the street
Auf dem Land sein	to be in the country
Auf dem Weg	on the way
Bestehen auf	to insist on

(v) *Aus*

Er kommt/stammt aus Berlin	he comes from Berlin
Aus Holz (usw)	made of wood (etc.)
Bestehen aus	to consist of

(vi) *Ausgenommen*

Alle sind artig, ihn ausge- nommen	all are well-behaved except him

47

(vii) *Außer*

Außer dir sehe ich niemand	I see nobody except you
Er ist außer Atem	he is out of breath
Er ist außer sich (vor)	he is beside himself (with)

(viii) *Außerhalb*

Das Haus lag außerhalb der Stadt.	the house lay outside the town

(ix) *Bei*

Er wohnt bei seinen Eltern	he lives with his parents
Bei schlechtem Wetter	in bad weather
Bei seiner Ankunft (Rückkehr)	on his arrival (return)
Bei dieser Gelegenheit	at this opportunity
Er hat kein Geld bei sich	he has no money on him
Bei Tagesanbruch	at dawn
Bei Sonnenuntergang	at sunset
Anwesend bei	present at
Sich beklagen bei	to complain to
Sich entschuldigen bei	to apologise to
Helfen bei	to help with

(x) *Bis*

Er bleibt bis Ostern	he is staying till Easter.
Bis nächsten Sonntag ist er zurück	he'll be back by next Sunday
Neun bis zehn (9—10) Jahre	nine to ten years
Er ging bis zum Rand der Klippe	he went to the edge of the cliff
Alle arbeiteten bis auf ihn	all were working except him

(xi) *Dank*

Dank deiner Bemühung	thanks to your efforts

(xii) *Diesseits*

Diesseits des Meeres	this side of the sea

(xiii) *Durch*

Er geht durch die Stadt	he walks through the town
Er wurde durch den Lärm geweckt	he was awakened by the noise

48

(xiv) *Entgegen*

Er kam mir entgegen	he came towards me

(xv) *Entlang*

Er ging die Straße entlang	he walked along the street

(xvi) *Für*

Er tat es für mich	he did it for me
Jahr für Jahr	year after year
Danken für	to thank for
Sich interessieren für	to be interested in
Schwärmen für	to be very keen on
Sorgen für	to look after
Gelten für	to be considered
Er gilt für einen Narren	he is considered a fool
Halten für	to consider
Ich halte es für überflüssig	I consider it unnecessary

(xvii) *Gegen*

Wir flogen gegen den Wind	we flew against the wind
Gegen 4 Uhr	about four o'clock
Gegen Ende des Jahres	towards the end of the year
Ich bin nichts gegen ihn	I'm nothing compared with him
Freundlich gegen	friendly towards
Sich wehren gegen	to oppose
Etwas/nichts dagegen haben	to have something/nothing against it

(xviii) *Gegenüber*

Er wohnt dem Kino gegenüber	he lives opposite the cinema

(xix) *Gemäß*

Seiner Pflicht gemäß	according to his duty

(xx) *Hinter* + *accusative*

Er ging hinter das Haus	he went behind the house

(xxi) *Hinter* + *dative*

Er versteckte sich hinter dem Schrank	he was hiding behind the cupboard

(xxii) *In* + *accusative*

Ins Ausland reisen	to go abroad
Ins Freie gehen	to go into the open air
Ins Theater (usw) gehen	to go to the theatre etc.
In Ordnung bringen	to tidy
Ich schnitt mich in die Hand	I cut my hand
Eingewickelt in	wrapped in
Verliebt in	in love with
Einfallen in	to attack
Einsteigen in	to get on (trains etc.)
Eintreten in	to enter
Geraten in	to get into (difficulties etc.)

(xxiii) *In* + *dative*

In der Nähe von	near
Im Freien sein	to be in the open air
In der Nacht	at night
Im Augenblick	at the moment
In dem Augenblick	at that moment
Einmal im Jahre	once a year
Im Gegenteil	on the contrary
Im allgemeinen	in general
Im Radio/Fernsehen	on the wireless/television
In einer Entfernung von	at a distance of
In Gegensatz zu	in contrast to
Ankommen in	to arrive at
Bestehen in	to consist in

(xxiv) *Inmitten*

Inmitten der Bäume	among the trees

(xxv) *Innerhalb*

Innerhalb der Stadt	inside the town
Innerhalb eines Jahres	within a year

(xxvi) *Jenseits*

Jenseits des Meeres	on the other side of the sea

(xxvii) *Kraft*

Kraft seines Ranges	by virtue of his rank

(xxviii) *Mit*

Er kam mit mir	he came with me
Mit Tinte (Bleistift) geschrieben	written in ink (pencil)
Mit Absicht	intentionally
Mit dem Auto (usw)	by car (etc.)
Mit leiser (lauter) Stimme	in a quiet (loud) voice
Fertig mit	finished with
Sich beschäftigen mit	to be busy with
Mit dem Kopf nicken	to nod one's head
Rechnen mit	to count on
Mit dem Schwanz wedeln	to wag its tail
Sprechen mit	to talk to
Umgehen mit	to associate with

(xxix) *(Ver) mittels*

Mittels seiner Hilfe	with his aid

(xxx) *Nach*

Er fuhr nach Berlin	he went to Berlin
Er ging nach Hause	he went home
Nach einer Stunde	after an hour
Nach meiner Meinung } Meiner Meinung nach }	in my opinion
Der Reihe nach	in turn
Allem Anschein nach	to all appearances
In der Richtung nach	in the direction of
Sich erkundigen nach } Fragen nach }	to enquire about
Schicken nach	to send for
Schmecken nach	to taste of
Urteilen nach	to judge from
Riechen nach	to smell of
Gierig nach	eager for

(xxxi) *Neben* + *accusative*

Er stellte sich neben das Fenster	he went and stood near the window

(xxxii) **Neben** + *dative*
Er stand neben dem Fenster   he was standing by the window

(xxxiii) **Ohne**
Ohne seine Frau fuhr er nach   he went to America without his
   Amerika   wife

(xxxiv) **Seit**
Seit dem Krieg   since the war
Seit zwei Jahren lerne ich   I have been learning German for
   Deutsch*   two years
Ich wartete seit langem*   I had been waiting for a long time

(xxxv) **(An) statt**
Er tat es statt meiner   he did it instead of me
Statt des Weins trank er   he drank beer instead of wine
   Bier

(xxxvi) **Trotz**
Trotz des Wetters   despite the weather
(N.B. **Trotzdem:** nevertheless)

(xxxvii) **Über** + *accusative*
Er ging über die Brücke   he went over the bridge
Er fuhr über Berlin   he went via Berlin
Ein Bericht über   a report on
Froh über   glad about
Traurig über   sad about
Enttäuscht über   disappointed in
Erstaunt über   surprised at
Zornig über   angry at
Sich beklagen über   to complain about
Sich freuen über   to be glad about
Klagen über   to complain of
Lachen über   to laugh at
Sich wundern über   to be surprised at
Schreiben über   to write about

*See p 34.

52

(xxxviii) *Über* + *dative*

| Die Möwen kreisten über dem Schiff | the seagulls circled over the ship |

(xxxix) *Um*

Um die Stadt	round the town
Um 4 Uhr	at 4 o'clock
Um so besser	all the better
Um so mehr	all the more
Bitten um	to ask for
Bringen um	to rob of
Sich handeln um	be a question of
Sich kümmern um	to worry about

(xl) *Um ... willen*

| Um Gottes willen | for heaven's sake |

(xli) *Unter* + *accusative*

| Er ging unter die Brücke | he walked under the bridge |

(xlii) *Unter* + *dative*

Unter den Kindern	among the children
Unter anderm	among other things
Unter dieser Bedingung	on this condition
Unter diesen Umständen	in these circumstances
Unter der Regierung von	in the reign of
Unter uns	amongst ourselves

(xliii) *Unterhalb*

| Unterhalb der Brücke wird der Fluß breiter | the river widens below the bridge |

(xliv) *Unweit*

| Unweit des Dorfes lag der Bauernhof | the farm lay not far from the village |

(xlv) *Von*

Von Zeit zu Zeit	from time to time
Von nun an	from now on
Abhängig von	dependent on
Nördlich (usw) von	to the north (etc.) of
Von Ansehen kennen	to know by sight

Erzählen von ⎫ Sagen von ⎭	to tell of
Abhalten von	to keep, prevent from
Abhängen von	to depend on
Sprechen von	to talk of
Weichen von	to budge from

(xlvi) *Vor* + *accusative*

Er stellte sich vor das Fenster	he went and stood in front of the window

(xlvii) *Vor* + *dative*

Vor einem Jahr	a year ago
Vor langer Zeit	a long time ago
Vor allen Dingen ⎫ Vor allem ⎭	above all
Blaß vor	pale with
Sicher vor	safe from
Draußen vor	outside
Angst haben vor ⎫ Sich fürchten vor ⎭	to be afraid of
Vor Freude Lachen	to laugh with joy
Schützen vor	to protect against
Warnen vor	to warn against
Weichen vor	to give way to
Weinen vor	to cry for
Vor Angst (usw) Zittern	to tremble with fear (etc.)

(xlviii) *Während*

Während der Sommerferien	during the summer holidays

(xlix) *Wegen*

Wegen des Wetters	because of the weather
Berühmt wegen	famous for
Loben wegen	to praise for
Schelten wegen	to scold for
Sich schämen wegen	to be ashamed because of
Tadeln wegen	to blame for
N.B. Meinetwegen, deinet-wegen (usw)	for my sake, your sake, etc.

54

(l) *Wider*

Normally indicates mental or moral opposition

Er tat es wider meinen Willen he did it against my wish

Wider Willen   reluctantly

N.B. Verbs compounded with **wider** govern the dative (see p 29)

(li) *Zeit*

Zeit meines Lebens   during my life

(lii) *Zu*

Er ging zum Bahnhof	he went to the station
Er ging zur Schule	he went to school
Er ging zu Bett	he went to bed
Zu Hause	at home
Zu Fuß	on foot
Zu Ostern, Pfingsten, Weihnachten	at Easter, Whitsun, Christmas
Zu Mittag (Abend) essen	to have lunch (dinner)
Eine Briefmarke zu 30 Pf.	a 30 Pf. stamp
Zu beiden Seiten	on both sides
Zur Not	if need be
Zum Glück	fortunately
Zum Beispiel	for example
Das Gasthaus zum Löwen	the 'Lion' inn
Zu meinem Erstaunen	to my surprise
Bringen zu	to make, provoke
Gehören zu	to belong to (i.e. to be part of)
Verurteilen zu	to condemn to
Wählen zu	to elect
Werden zu	to become

(liii) *Zwischen* + *accusative*

Er setzte sich zwischen die beiden Jungen   he sat down between the two boys

(liv) *Zwischen* + *dative*

Er saß zwischen den beiden Jungen   he was sitting between the two boys

Miscellaneous

Indirect speech and question

(i) In indirect speech and question the verb is in the subjunctive (see p 22).

(ii) In an indirect question the verb is sent to the end of the clause.

(iii) The Germans prefer to omit the conjunction 'that' (**daß**) in indirect speech.

(iv) *Scheme of tenses*

In indirect speech the German should retain the same tense as the original direct speech, provided the subjunctive and indicative forms of the verb are different. If they are identical, the verb in the indirect speech is put back one tense in the past (e.g. present to imperfect).

e.g. *Direct Speech*   *Indirect Speech*

(a) **Er ist traurig**   **Er sagte, er sei traurig**

The forms are different so the present subjunctive is used in the indirect speech.

Ich habe ein Buch   **Er sagte, ich hätte** (not **habe**) **ein Buch**

The form of the present subjunctive would be identical to the present indicative, so the imperfect subjunctive is used.

(b) **Er hat die Aufgabe**   **Er sagte, er habe die Aufgabe gemacht**   **gemacht**

Perfect subjunctive because the forms are different.

Sie haben die Aufgabe   **Er sagte, sie hätten** (not **haben**) **gemacht**   **die Aufgabe gemacht**

Pluperfect, not perfect, because the forms are identical.

This may be summarised as follows (the tense in brackets is the one to be used if the indicative and subjunctive forms are identical):

Direct Speech	*Indirect Speech*
(a) Present Indicative	Present Subjunctive (Imperfect Subjunctive)
(b) Imperfect Indicative ⎫ Perfect Indicative ⎬ Pluperfect Indicative ⎭	Perfect Subjunctive (Pluperfect Subjunctive)
(c) Future Indicative ⎱ Conditional ⎰	Future Subjunctive (Conditional)

N.B. In an Indirect Question the word for 'if' is **ob**.

Conditional sentences

(i) *Types*

(a) **Wenn ich müde bin, so gehe ich zu Bett.** If I am tired I go to bed.

(b) **Wenn ich müde bin, so werde ich zu Bett gehen.** If I am tired I shall go to bed.

(c) **Wenn ich müde wäre,** {so würde ich zu Bett gehen. / so ginge ich zu Bett.

If I were tired I would go to bed.

(d) **Wenn ich müde gewesen wäre, so wäre ich zu Bett gegangen.** If I had been tired I would have gone to bed.

N.B. Word order!

In (a) and (b) the verbs are in the indicative.

In (c) and (d) the verbs are in the subjunctive.

In type (c) the conditional is normally used in the **so** clause and must be used if the subjunctive and indicative forms are identical.

Wenn *clause*	**So** *clause*
(a) Present Indicative	Present Indicative
(b) Present Indicative	Future Indicative
(c) Imperfect Subjunctive	{ Conditional / Imperfect Subjunctive
(d) Pluperfect Subjunctive	Pluperfect Subjunctive

57

(ii) *Omission of* **so** *and* **wenn**

(a) **Wenn** may be omitted if **so** is used.

e.g. **Bin ich müde, so gehe ich zu Bett.**

N.B. New word order — verb first.

(b) **So** may be omitted if **wenn** is used.

e.g. **Wenn ich müde bin, gehe ich zu Bett.**

(c) If the **so** clause precedes the **wenn** clause, **so** is omitted and normal word order applies.

e.g. **Ich gehe zu Bett, wenn ich müde bin.**

Word order

(i) *Verbs*

(a) The main verb must be the second idea in the sentence unless it is the imperative or interrogative form.

e.g. **Sie stehen um sieben Uhr auf.**

   Wenn es sieben Uhr ist, stehen Sie auf.

   Stehen Sie um sieben Uhr auf!

   Stehen Sie um sieben Uhr auf?

(b) Infinitives and past participles go to the end of the clause.

(c) Verbs go to the end of subordinate clauses (see section v).

(d) If there are two infinitives in a sentence and the finite verb is sent to the end then it will precede these infinitives.

e.g. **Ich weiß, daß er wird kommen können.**

   Er sagte, daß er das Buch nicht habe finden können.

(ii) *Nicht*

Nicht goes as near the end of the sentence as possible unless it is making a particular word negative when it precedes that word.

e.g. **Ich kann ihn nicht sehen** I cannot see him.

   Ich kann ihn nicht heute sehen I cannot see him today.

(iii) *Adverbs* (see p 43)

   1. Time   2. Manner   3. Place

e.g. **Jeden Tag fährt er mit dem Bus in die Schule.**

If two or more adverbs of the same type occur in a sentence the more general precedes the more specific.

e.g. **Er kommt jeden Tag um 4 Uhr nach Hause.**

(iv) *Objects*

(a) If both the direct and indirect objects are nouns the indirect precedes the direct.

e.g. **Er gibt dem Mann das Buch.**

(b) If they are both pronouns the direct precedes the indirect.

e.g. **Er gibt es ihm.**

(c) If one is a noun and the other a pronoun the pronoun always comes first.

e.g. **Er gibt ihm das Buch.   Er gibt es dem Mann.**

(v) *Conjunctions*

(a) *Coordinating*, i.e. do not affect word order.

aber but	**oder** or
allein but (literary)	**sondern** but
denn for	**und** and

e.g. **Ich will zu Bett gehen, denn ich bin müde.**

N.B. **Sondern** and not **aber** must be used when

    (i)   The preceding clause is negative.

    (ii) Both clauses have the same subject.

    (iii) The second clause directly contradicts the first, e.g. **Sie sind nicht reich, aber glücklich** but **Sie sind nicht reich, sondern arm.**

(b) *Adverbial*, i.e. require inversion of verb and subject.

also		**dennoch**	yet, nevertheless
so	therefore,	**(je)doch**	
daher	and so	**deswegen**	that is why, therefore.
darum		**deshalb**	
auch	also, too	**indessen**	
auch . . . nicht	nor, neither	**inzwischen**	meanwhile
außerdem	besides,	**unterdessen**	
übrigens	moreover	**kaum**	hardly, scarcely
da	then, so	**sonst**	otherwise, else
dann	then (i.e. next)	**trotzdem**	in spite of that
		und zwar	in fact

e.g. **Es war kalt, deswegen sind wir zu Hause geblieben.**
    Wir müssen eilen, sonst verpassen wir den Zug.

(c) *Subordinating*, i.e. send the verb to the end of the clause.
Almost all conjunctions other than those listed in (a) and (b) are subordinating.

e.g. **Weil es kalt war, trug er ein Paar Handschuhe. Ich wußte, daß er zu Hause war.**

Numerals

(i) *Cardinal numbers*

1	eins	21	einundzwanzig
2	zwei	22.	zweiundzwanzing, etc.
3	drei	30	dreißig
4	vier	31	einunddreißig, etc.
5	fünf	40	vierzig
6	sechs	50	fünfzig
7	sieben	60	*sechzig*
8	acht	70	*siebzig*
9	neun	80	achtzig
10	zehn	90	neunzig
11	elf	100	hundert
12	zwölf	101	hunderteins, etc.
13	dreizehn	110	hundertzehn, etc.
14	vierzehn	200	zweihundert, etc.
15	fünfzehn	1,000	tausend
16	*sechzehn*	1,001	tausendeins, etc.
17	*siebzehn*	2,200	zweitausend zweihundert
18	achtzehn	1,000,000	eine Million
19	neunzehn		
20	zwanzig		

(ii) *Ordinal numbers*

1—19: add *-te* to the cardinal number, e.g. **der zweite**, except for **eins — der erste   drei — der dritte   acht — der achte**

20 and over add *-ste* to the cardinal numbers
e.g. **der dreiunddreißigste**

101 and over start again, e.g. **der hundertzweite, der hundertzwanzigste.**

(iii) *Fractions*, etc.

1/3 **ein Drittel**   1/4 **ein Viertel** etc. (all neuter), but 1/2 **die Hälfte**
1/2 **halb**

N.B. half an apple **ein halber Apfel**
half the apple **die Hälfte des Apfels**
1½ **anderthalb** or **eineinhalb**
2½ **zweieinhalb**, etc.
-times *-mal* e.g. **einmal, zweimal**, etc.
-ly, **erstens, zweitens**, etc.
-fold *-fach*, e.g. **einfach, zweifach**, etc.

kinds of *-erlei*, e.g. **einerlei, zweierlei**, etc. N.B. **allerlei** all
kinds of

Time

Wie spät ist es? **Wieviel Uhr ist es?** }	What is the time?

1.00	**es ist eins**
	es ist ein Uhr
1.05	**es ist fünf (Minuten) nach eins**
	es ist ein Uhr fünf
1.15	**es ist Viertel zwei***
	es ist Viertel nach eins
	es ist ein Uhr fünfzehn
1.30	**es ist halb zwei***
	es ist ein Uhr dreißig
1.40	**es ist zwanzig (Minuten) vor zwei**
	es ist ein Uhr vierzig
1.45	**es ist dreiviertel zwei***
	es ist Viertel vor zwei
	es ist ein Uhr fünfundvierzig
1.59	**es ist eine Minute vor zwei**
	es ist ein Uhr neunundfünfzig

to **vor**   past **nach**
12 noon **Mittag; zwölf Uhr**
12 midnight **Mitternacht; vierundzwanzig Uhr**

---

*N.B. The differences between the English — quarter past *one* — and the
German — quarter *two*, etc.

a.m. **morgens, vormittags**.

p.m. **nachmittags** (up to *c.* 6 p.m.)

abends (up to *c.* 10 p.m.)

nachts (after *c.* 10 p.m., including the early hours of the morning which can also be **morgens**)

N.B. at 1 o'clock **um ein Uhr**

about 1 o'clock **gegen ein Uhr, etwa um ein Uhr**

am Tag by day

am Morgen
am Vormittag } in the morning

am Nachmittag in the afternoon

am Abend in the evening

BUT **in der Nacht** at night.

Dates

Days (all masc.)		*Months* (all masc.)	
Monday	**Montag**	January	**Januar**
Tuesday	**Dienstag**	February	**Februar**
Wednesday	**Mittwoch**	March	**März**
Thursday	**Donnerstag**	April	**April**
Friday	**Freitag**	May	**Mai**
Saturday	**Samstag**	June	**Juni**
	Sonnabend	July	**Juli**
Sunday	**Sonntag**	August	**August**
		September	**September**
		October	**Oktober**
		November	**November**
		December	**Dezember**

Der wievielte ist es heute?
Den wievielten haben wir heute? } What is the date today?
Welches Datum haben wir heute?

Dates are formed, as in English, by using ordinal numbers (see p 60)

N.B. these numbers are adjectives and must be declined

e.g. **Heute ist der erste Januar (der 1. Januar)**
Heute haben wir den ersten Januar (den 1. January).

N.B. On Monday *Am* **Montag**
On 2nd July *Am* **zweiten (2.)** *Juli*
In July *Im* **Juli**
In 1939 *Im* **Jahre 1939** or **1939** (never **in 1939**)

Weak masculine nouns

(a) *Adding -n*
e.g. **der Junge**

	Singular	*Plural*
N.	**der Junge**	**die Jungen**
A.	**den Jungen**	**die Jungen**
G.	**des Jungen**	**der Jungen**
D.	**dem Jungen**	**den Jungen**

Some common nouns in this group:

der Affe monkey	**der Kunde** customer
der Bauer farmer	**der Löwe** lion
der Bote messenger	**der Matrose** sailor
der Erbe heir	**der Neffe** nephew
der Franzose Frenchman	**der Riese** giant
der Geselle companion	**der Sklave** slave
der Knabe boy	

N.B. **Der Herr** + *-n* in the singular, + *-en* in the plural.

(b) *Adding -en*
e.g. **der Mensch**

	Singular	*Plural*
N.	**der Mensch**	**die Menschen**
A.	**den Menschen**	**die Menschen**
G.	**des Menschen**	**der Menschen**
D.	**dem Menschen**	**den Menschen**

Some common nouns in this group:

der Bär bear	**der Ochs** ox
der Elefant elephant	**der Prinz** prince
der Fürst prince	**der Polizist** policeman
der Held hero	**der Soldat** soldier
der Kamerad comrade	**der Student** student

(c) *Adding* **-n** *and* **-ns**
e.g. **der Name.**

	Singular	Plural
N.	der Name	die Namen
A.	den Namen	die Namen
G.	des Namens	der Namen
D.	dem Namen	den Namen

Some common nouns in this group:

der Friede peace   **der Haufe(n)** heap

der Gedanke thought   **der Wille** will

der Glaube belief

(d) *Das Herz*

	Singular	Plural
N.	das Herz	die Herzen
A.	das Herz	die Herzen
G.	des Herzens	der Herzen
D.	dem Herzen	den Herzen

Nouns in apposition

A noun should be in the same case as the noun or pronoun with which it
stands in apposition.

e.g. **Mein Freund, der Lehrer, wohnt hier**

Kennen Sie meinen Freund, den Lehrer?

Das ist das Haus meines Freundes, des Lehrers

Ich sprach mit meinem Freund, dem Lehrer

Sie kamen am Montag, dem 20. Juli

Ein Dutzend Bücher

Mit einem Dutzend Büchern

Eine Tasse heißer Kaffee (or heißen Kaffees)

Note the following cases of apposition:

Die Stadt Berlin the city of Berlin

Luther ging auf die Universität Erfurt Luther went to the University of Erfurt

Eine Besichtigung der Festung Ehrenbreitstein a visit to the
fortress of Ehrenbreitstein

Im Monat Mai in the month of May